AF426382

Nahum's Book About Numbers

By Nahum Edwards

Illustrated by Muniba Khan

0 Zero

I see zero foot prints in the snow.

1 One

I see one snowman in the snow.

I see two Christmas trees
in the snow.

3 Three

I see three snowballs
in the snow.

4 Four

I see four snow tunnels in the snow.

I see five kids playing in the snow.

6 Six

I see six snowflakes in the snow.

7 Seven

I see seven cars in the snow.

8 Eight

I see eight bins in the snow.

9 Nine

I see nine sticks in the snow.

10 Ten

I see ten hats in the snow.

11 Eleven

I see eleven candy canes
in the snow.

12 Twelve

I see twelve pine cones
in the snow.

13 Thirteen

I see thirteen handprints in the snow.

14 Fourteen

I see fourteen penguins in the snow.

15 Fifteen

I see fifteen pumpkins in the snow.

16 Sixteen

I see sixteen ice skates
in the snow.

17 Seventeen

I see seventeen gingerbread houses in the snow.

18 Eighteen

I see eighteen snowboards
in the snow.

19 Nineteen

I see nineteen sweaters
in the snow.

20 Twenty

I see twenty icicles on a tree in the snow.

About the Author

Nahum Edwards is a five year old boy who lives in Pennsylvania with his mom, brothers, sister, and dad. Nahum is a brave, adventurous, and creative kid. Nahum once told his mom that when he grows up he wants to be an author, engineer, Illustrator, and a soccer player. Nahum's mom told him "You do not have to be a grown-up to accomplish your goals, in fact you could start right now." Nahum was fascinated by what his mom told him. He is practicing soccer, and doing small engineering projects at home. Nahum wrote three books,and he is excited to share this one with you.